RM70:
SEVENTY YEARS OF
A LONDON ICON

MALCOLM BATTEN

AMBERLEY

First published 2024

Amberley Publishing
The Hill, Stroud
Gloucestershire, GL5 4EP

www.amberley-books.com

Copyright © Malcolm Batten, 2024

The right of Malcolm Batten to be identified
as the Author of this work has been asserted in
accordance with the Copyrights, Designs and
Patents Act 1988.

ISBN 978 1 3981 2361 8 (print)
ISBN 978 1 3981 2362 5 (ebook)

British Library Cataloguing in Publication Data.
A catalogue record for this book is available from
the British Library.

Origination by Amberley Publishing.
Printed in the UK.

Contents

Introduction

The Routemaster bus has become synonymous with London and is recognised the world over. Although fewer were built than of the preceding RT type, their uniqueness and longevity made them instantly recognizable as the typical London bus. A new design was first conceived as a replacement for the trolleybuses where the electrical supply equipment was reaching the end of its economic life, as well as the need to replace the vehicles themselves. Almost all trolleybuses were seventy-seat six-wheelers. Tests had shown that around sixty-four passengers was the maximum a conductor could collect fares from over short distances, so that was the target capacity for the new bus design.

The prototype was unveiled in 1954. Although the body was a conventional open rear platform design, there were many advanced mechanical features. A conventional chassis was replaced by two sub-frames. There was an independent suspension system, automatic air-operated gearbox, power steering (added in 1957) and hydraulic brakes. The sixty-four passengers could be carried in a vehicle weighing the same as a fifty-six-seat RT type.

RM1 had a Park Royal body and AEC AV590 9.6-litre engine. When originally exhibited at the 1954 Commercial Motor Show it had a horizontal underfloor radiator and was 27 feet long by 8 feet wide. It was modified in 1957 with a front-mounted radiator which increased the length by 4 inches. RM2 followed in 1955 and was originally fitted with a smaller 7.7-litre engine which was soon replaced. It was painted green and trialled at Reigate on route 406 in 1957. It was shortly afterwards repainted red and sent to Turnham Green garage for route 91. Two other prototypes emerged in 1957. RML3 (later RM3) had a Leyland 0.600 engine and Weymann body to a similar design as RM2, while CRL4 (later RMC4) had a Leyland engine and ECW body with rear doors and was in Green Line livery. 'Pre-production' RMs 5–8 came in 1958–9 with AEC engines and Park Royal bodies.

The prototypes were registered SLT56-9. However, RM 5 upwards had registrations matching their fleet numbers, e.g. RM5-300 were VLT 5-300.

Main production of AEC/Park Royal Routemasters started in 1959 and the first full entry to service was on 11 November 1959 when RMs began to replace trolleybuses at West Ham and Poplar. Further batches entered service, with the last trolleybuses being replaced at Fulwell in May 1962.

The first variation to the type came in 1961. 30-foot-long two-axle buses had been legalised since 1956 and were in common use outside London. The first 30-foot Routemasters, RML880–903 (originally to be ER880–903), were created by inserting an extra 2-foot 4-inch section in the middle. These were sent to Finchley for route 104.

Front entrance double-deckers were increasingly becoming popular outside London, and in an attempt to popularise Routemaster sales to other operators a 30-foot front entrance vehicle, RMF1254, was built in 1962. Although this never ran in public service with London Transport, it was shown at the 1962 Commercial Motor Show and demonstrated to Manchester, Liverpool and East Kent. However, the only other company to purchase Routemasters was Northern General who took fifty with front entrances and Leyland engines.

RMC 1453–1520 were production Green Line vehicles in 1962–3 with twin headlights, rear doors and air suspension at the rear. Standard RMs then followed up to RM2217 in 1965, around a quarter being fitted with Leyland engines. A batch of 30-foot-long Green Line vehicles, RCL2218–60, followed in 1965, these having a more powerful AEC AV690 11.3-litre engine. These were followed by 500 more RMLs 2261-2760 from 1965–8 of which RML2306–55 and 2411–60 were green buses for the Country Area.

The only other Routemasters to be built were sixty-five short front-entrance buses for the contract that London Transport operated on behalf of British European Airways in 1966–7. These towed a two-wheeled luggage trailer.

One-man operation of double-deck buses had been allowed since 1966 and for this the rear engine bus with entrance alongside the driver had an advantage. The Leyland Atlantean had been the first rear engine bus to enter production in 1958 and had found favour in many fleets. In 1965–6 London Transport took fifty Atlanteans (XA class) and eight of the rival Daimler Fleetline (XF class) for comparison trials. In 1966 they also built an experimental rear engine derivative of the Routemaster, FRM1. The Park Royal body used around 60 per cent of the components of the RM. Originally five were to be built with three as demonstrators, but with the disappointing sales of the Routemaster outside London and with British Leyland already offering the Atlantean, Fleetline and Bristol VR, it was considered that this would not be viable and FRM1 was to remain unique.

In 1966 London Transport announced the Bus Reshaping Plan. One-person operation (OPO) would become the standard for future new designs, with crew operation (and therefore the Routemasters) to be eliminated by 1978, a mere ten years after the last had been built. Under the Reshaping Plan, only single-deck buses were bought in 1968–70, and then Daimler Fleetlines from 1971.

In 1967 the government introduced a grants scheme. Grants of up to 75 per cent would be available for capital investment in such facilities as bus stations, and local authorities could subsidise rural bus services, to which the government would contribute 50 per cent. Furthermore, grants of 25 per cent were offered on the purchase of vehicles suitable for one-person operation. This grant was to lead to the cessation in manufacture of the traditional half-cab crew-operated double-decker by 1970. The last batch of RMLs entered service on 1 March 1968. The very last numerically, RML 2760, was sent to Upton Park to join the allocation on route 15. As the last Routemaster, it was inevitable that it would become something of a celebrity vehicle.

The Country Area green and Green Line buses would be transferred to a new company, London Country Bus Services, from 1 January 1970 when this part of London Transport passed to the National Bus Company. However, when LCBS brought in new one-person-operated vehicles these were sold back to London Transport. Meanwhile the Central Area red buses, though still titled 'London Transport', now moved from being under direct state control to that of the Greater London Council.

From 29 June 1984, a new organisation, London Regional Transport, took over London Transport from the GLC. Then from 1 April 1985 a new wholly owned subsidiary, London Buses Ltd took on the operation of buses. The Labour-controlled GLC had fallen foul of the Conservative government of Margaret Thatcher and would be abolished in March 1986.

The Conservatives also passed the 1985 Transport Act which introduced deregulation whereby the old system of route licensing was replaced by allowing open competition on commercially registered routes and competitive tendering elsewhere. London was spared competition, but LRT was required to put routes out to competitive tender. The National Bus Company fleets were all privatised between July 1986 and April 1988, some like London Country being split into smaller units first.

Some 200 standard RMs had already been withdrawn before deregulation was introduced in 1985, but this now increased rapidly. Those with Leyland engines had mostly gone by 1990. New OPO double-deck buses replaced some, others went as routes were lost on tendering. Also, minibuses had become a national rage and many of these entered London service, even replacing Routemasters on some routes such as the 28 and 31.

However, at an age when they might have been expected to go to scrap, many operators turned to the RM as a way to compete or to fight off potential competition. Routemasters, up to now only found in the London Transport area and the North East, were now entering service all over the country, with many initially going to Scotland. Others were sold abroad for service, while they also found favour for non-PSV uses such as hospitality and promotional vehicles.

In 1988 LRT announced that no further routes would be converted to OPO until boarding times could be improved, thus the twenty-five remaining Routemaster-operated routes would survive into the next decade. These were trunk routes into Central London where it was found that OPO caused congestion and longer journey times.

In April 1989 London Buses were split into eleven regional operating units, plus London Coaches who ran the sightseeing services. This was in preparation for eventual privatisation in the 1990s. Buses carried the name of the local unit, e.g. London Forest, and a local emblem.

When privatisation did take place in 1994, it was the intention that no one purchaser should be able to buy adjacent operating districts. However, there was no such proviso regarding the selling on of privatised companies or the purchase of other companies providing tendered services. Eventually the four main national groups – Arriva, First Group, Go-Ahead Group and Stagecoach – all gained multiple areas of London, although there were also other players.

London Regional Transport was replaced by a new body, London Transport Buses who would now administer route tendering amongst other things. One stipulation by them in 1994 was that buses on routes entering Central London must maintain a 75 per cent (later 80 per cent) red livery, so the national liveries of Arriva, First and Stagecoach would not be seen in London on the Routemasters they had inherited.

A refurbishment programme was made to the RMLs from 1992 to extend their lives by at least ten years. New engines by Cummins or Iveco had already replaced many of the AEC or Leyland originals as these companies were no longer in business. Now it was the turn of the interiors to be refurbished with new seat coverings and improvements made to heating and handrails. However, the use of Routemasters on Sundays was phased out in 1992 by LRT in favour of one-person operation.

In the latter half of the decade, accessibility became the watchword following the passing of the Disability Discrimination Act 1995. Low-floor single-deck buses with wheelchair and buggy access began to enter service. In late 1998, the first wheelchair-accessible double-deckers entered service on Arriva's route 242. By the end of 1999 there were over 500 running in Greater London, and the 1,000 mark had been reached before the end of year 2000.

The new Millennium coincided with a change in ownership for London's bus services. From 3 July 2000 a new Mayor of London was appointed, who took over responsibility for London Bus Services Ltd and a new regulatory authority called Transport for London (TfL). The first London Mayor was none other than Ken Livingstone, the former leader of the Greater London Council.

London had almost uniquely retained crew operation with Routemasters on certain trunk routes through Central London. Initially this seemed set to continue and indeed increase. In 2000 TfL started sourcing former Routemasters which were then refurbished by Marshalls of Cambridge. A total of twenty-one refurbished RMs were put on route 13, replacing RMLs which were redistributed to other routes. But all good things must come to an end and on 30 September 2002 the Mayor announced that Routemasters would be replaced on all the then remaining twenty routes. The reasons were due to the proposed introduction of the 'Oyster' smartcards making conductors unnecessary and increasing pressure from disabled groups for accessible buses. First to go were the Routemasters serving route 15 Paddington–Blackwall on 29 August 2003. RML2760, the last RML numerically, had been on the route for most of its life since 1968. The other routes followed through 2003–5. These last days would be marked by the appearance of 'guest' vehicles from operators and the enthusiast fraternity. For the last day of route 8, London Transport Museum brought out RM1, carrying paying passengers for the first time since 1959!

On Friday 9 December 2005 route 159 Marble Arch–Streatham was converted as the last Routemaster-worked route. The Routemasters were phased out through the lunchtime period with the last scheduled departure from Marble Arch at 12.10. This was worked by RM 2217, the last-built short RM, which was due to reach Brixton garage at 13.30. Because of the crowds who turned out for the last day it arrived over half an hour late at 14.07. Actually, although this was the official last bus, RM54, which had been the last to run right through to Streatham station, had equally been held up by the crowds and did not reach the terminus until 14.08, making it the last Routemaster in normal service!

However, this was not to mean the end of Routemaster operation altogether in London. On 14 November 2005 a pair of heritage routes were launched using RMs. The 15, worked by Stagecoach, ran between Tower Hill and Trafalgar Square and heritage route 9, worked by First, ran between Aldwych and Royal Albert Hall. The 9 was withdrawn in 2014. The 15 ran until September 2019, thus bringing to an end the regular running of Routemasters by London Transport and its successors. However, some of the London bus companies including Go-Ahead retained a few Routemasters as heritage vehicles or for special commercial duties.

Some of the last Routemasters were replaced by Mercedes-Benz Citaro 'bendy-buses' then being introduced. These proved unpopular, not least because of their scope for fare evasion. New London Mayor Boris Johnson promised to get rid of them and introduced a competition to design a new bus for London – a 'New Routemaster'. Some of the designs submitted featured the traditional RM radiator grille. However, the winning design eventually built by Wrightbus had little in common with its namesake except for a rear entrance/exit and (initially) a conductor. 1,000 of these 'New Routemasters', also known as the 'New Bus for London', were built for TfL before incoming Mayor Sadiq Khan axed further production.

This book does not set out to be a definitive history of the Routemaster. That has already been done by other authors. Instead, it is a photographic tribute to a bus that was designed specifically for London. At first it found little favour elsewhere. But later on, when most buses of that age would be going for scrap, many had a second career with operators around the country. Now, seventy years since the prototype first emerged, some Routemasters can still be found on sightseeing work in London, where their versality had enabled them to be not only open-topped but also lengthened. Others are in use for corporate hospitality, film work and wedding hires. Hundreds also survive in preservation, both in museum collections and with private owners. The London Transport Museum has prototypes RM1 and RM2, along with RM1737, RCL2229 and the unique FRM1. The London Bus Museum has RM3 (as RML3), RM140, RMC1461 and RML2760. Many of the preserved Routemasters can be seen at the various bus rallies, garage Open Days and route Running Days held each year along with other London types earlier and later. The term 'icon' is much maligned but if ever a bus deserved such a status this must be the one that qualifies.

Photographs are by the author except where indicated.

The Prototypes

RM1 as originally built in 1954 and before the registration plates had been fitted. (Photo by Colin Tait/©TfL from the London Transport Museum collection)

RM1 first entered public service on route 2 Golders Green–Crystal Palace on 8 February 1956. The blind boxes had been modified and the grille below the front blinds fitted by January 1955. This view shows it after the radiator was repositioned to the front in 1957. In 1959 it was retired to the training fleet. (Photo by Marcus Eavis/Online Transport Archive)

RM2 entered service in Country Area green livery on 20 May 1957 and was sent to Reigate for route 406. (Photographer unknown/©TfL from the London Transport Museum collection)

RM2 was soon repainted red. Here it is seen laying over while working on route 91 from Turnham Green garage (V) between 1957 and 1959, after which it was transferred to the training fleet. This garage was used for testing, being conveniently close to Chiswick Works. RMs 1 and 2 were transferred to the London Transport Museum in March 1985. (Photo by Harry Luff/Online Transport Archive)

RML3 was sent to Willesden for route 8, photographed in January 1958. This also was transferred to training duties in 1959 and renumbered RM3 in September 1961. (Photo by Dr Heinz Zimran/©TfL from the London Transport Museum collection)

CRL4 when working on trial from Romford garage (RE) on route 721 from 9 October 1957. This was renumbered RMC4 in August 1961. In 1964 it was rebuilt with a standard type of radiator and was the only one of the prototypes to remain in normal public service after 1959. (Photo by Peter Sykes/Online Transport Archive)

In Service with London Transport Until 1984

RM 514 when working from Highgate garage (now renamed Holloway) in original condition. RMs were allocated here from July 1960 to replace trolleybuses, route 239 having been trolleybus route 639. Note the 'Routemaster' name above the fleet number and the offside route number. Both these features were soon discontinued. (Photo by Julian Thompson/Online Transport Archive)

Fifteen early production Routemasters entered service from West Ham garage (WH) on 11 November 1959 to replace trolleybuses. The last trolleybuses from there finished in April 1960. Still in the area ten years later is RM97, seen at Stratford Broadway in June 1969 on local route 272. This has the full-size grille below the blind box unlike the later vehicle behind. The brake cooling grilles by the headlights have been filled in. RMs up to RM253 were built with non-opening upper-deck front windows.

RM191 stands at North Woolwich on 20 November 1969 with a short working of route 69 North Woolwich–Chingford Mount to Walthamstow Central station. The section from North Woolwich to Stratford had been part of trolleybus route 669 until February 1960. The pole to the right of the bus is a former trolleybus traction pole now in use as a lamp post. Note the grille below the blind box has been reduced in size to allow a full-width band – this was a modification made to Routemasters from 1963, as was fitting the triangular AEC-style badge on the radiator grille. Note also the advertisement for Red Rover tickets. These gave a day's travel on all Central Area red buses for 7 shillings (35p).

The RMC class were used on Green Line services from 1962, including the prototype CRL4 now renumbered RMC4. They replaced single-deck RFs and this avoided the need for duplication on some services. On 12 June 1969 RMC1497 stands at the Tilbury Ferry terminus of route 723 from London (Aldgate) in the company of RT4756 on route 370 to Romford. Both are allocated to Grays garage. From 1 January 1970 the green country buses and Green Line buses passed to the National Bus Company as London Country Bus Services.

The RCL class were delivered in June 1965 also for Green Line services, replacing RTs. Many went to Romford (RE) for the busy routes 721 and 722 from Aldgate to Brentwood or Corbets Tey near Upminster. They also worked on the seasonal route 726 to Whipsnade Zoo. RCL2220 stands at Aldgate. (Photo by R. C. Riley/Online Transport Archive)

Upton Park garage received a large batch of RMLs in 1966 for trunk route 15. Many routes had Sunday variations or extensions and in 1969 route 40 ran right through from Wanstead station to Norwood Junction on Sundays. On 8 June 1969 RML2523 takes a break from its normal weekday duties on the 15 as it stands at the Wanstead terminus of the 40 in Woodbine Place.

The first Routemasters for Country Area bus services were delivered in 1965. One hundred RMLs would be supplied in green, Nos RML 2306–55 and 2411–60. RML2347 stands at Forest Row station, terminus of the long route 409 from West Croydon, in October 1966. The route was cut back to East Grinstead in October 1979. (Photo by Marcus Eavis/Online Transport Archive)

A pair of new Routemasters in May 1966. They carry garage codes for Northfleet (NF) where they will be employed on the trunk route 480 Erith–Gravesend. However, RML2446 has blinds fitted for a special service on route 410 between Bromley North station and Biggin Hill International Air Fair. (Photo by Marcus Eavis/Online Transport Archive)

Green Line routes could be very popular at weekends and bank holidays, requiring relief buses, especially to Windsor. Harlow garage have put RML2444 on a relief 718 journey and this is rounding Marble Arch on its way back home. (Photo by R. C. Riley/Online Transport Archive)

Leyton garage's RM207 sports the white band introduced in 1972 and solid white roundel and white fleet numbers introduced in April 1974. The front upstairs windows are opening – the original body with non-opening windows has been replaced by a later one at overhaul. The rear wheel discs have been removed as this feature was discontinued. Note also the extended advertising panel. Green Park, 24 May 1984.

In the late 1970s/early 1980s some garages unofficially turned out buses with modified liveries as rally showbuses. Most of these were Routemasters given original-style features. One such was RM1000 with its unique 100 BXL registration. Note the gold underlined fleetname, brake cooling grilles, divided cream band and rear wheel discs. This was entered from South Croydon garage to the Norwich Rally held on 13 September 1981. There was quite a rivalry to see who could come up with the best-presented bus. However, London Buses Ltd banned this practice in 1985 when they succeeded London Transport.

The Routemasters, like their RT predecessors, were designed to have interchangeable jig-built bodies. They were overhauled at the Aldenham Works where the bodies would be separated from the frames and overhauled in a separate area. Overhead cranes were used to move the bodies around, as seen at the Open Day held on 25 September 1983 as part of the London Transport fifty years celebrations.

The bodies would be placed in these tilting rigs, which allowed full access to the underside. When London Transport bought 'off-the-peg' models like the Fleetlines, these were not designed for body interchangeability and Aldenham Works closed in 1986.

The mechanical parts of an RM – the front and rear subframes await the mounting of a newly overhauled body.

FRM1

In 1979 London Transport marked 150 years of London Buses with a series of events. One of these was a rally of vehicles through the ages held in Hyde Park on 8 July. Amongst the entries was FRM1. When first built it was trialled against the XA class Atlanteans on route 76 from Tottenham. Since 1978 it had been allocated to Stockwell garage for the Round London Sightseeing Tour – just visible on the blind display.

In 1981 FRM1 received an overhaul and was repainted in original style with cream band and gold underlined fleetname. It is seen at St Paul's Cathedral on 19 September 1981. It would remain on this work until withdrawn for preservation by the London Transport Museum in February 1983.

British European Airways/British Airways

London Transport operated a contract service for British European Airways between their air terminal at Gloucester Road and Heathrow Airport. AEC Regal IV coaches were used but larger aircraft required larger-capacity vehicles. The unique front-entrance Routemaster RMF1254, after its use as a demonstrator, was placed on the BEA contract and fitted with a towing hook for a luggage trailer. It did not get repainted but received dedicated adverts for BEA. It is seen at Heathrow with one of the AEC Regal IV coaches behind. (Photo by Harry Luff/Online Transport Archive)

Following the successful operation of RMF1254, in 1966–7 sixty-five short front-entrance Routemasters replaced the AEC Regal IV coaches on the contract service. Three of these, with NMY 630E nearest, are seen at Gloucester Road on 8 June 1969.

NMY 628E stands at Heathrow on 16 February 1970. They conveyed luggage in a two-wheeled trailer towed by the bus. Note the illuminated side BEA panel which was located on both sides of the bus.

BEA changed their livery to the then fashionable orange and white and NMY 639E sports the new colours on 24 August 1970. The illuminated side panels have been removed.

BEA merged with BOAC (British Overseas Airways Corporation) on 1 April 1974 to become British Airways. Some of the Routemasters received the new identity, as here in May 1974. The side adverts varied promoting different flight offers. Only thirty-eight Routemasters remained and not all had been repainted when the service was withdrawn in March 1979 following the extension of the Underground Piccadilly line to Heathrow.

Northern General

Northern General No. 3084, RCN 700, lays over in Newcastle on 26 July 1978. NBC standard National red had replaced the original maroon livery. The fifty Routemasters were new in 1964–5 and were all withdrawn between October 1976 and December 1980.

While most of the Northern General buses, including Routemasters, were in National red, some were painted yellow for use on routes that lay within the Tyne & Wear Passenger Transport Executive area. Inevitably these would stray onto other routes and No. 3109 is at the former Worswick Street bus station in Newcastle loading for Washington in September 1976.

London Transport's unique RMF1254 was fitted with a Leyland engine and joined the Northern fleet as No. 2154 in November 1966. Now as No. 3129, it is seen in Gateshead en route to Sunderland from Newcastle on 26 July 1978. The blind box has been modified to the style of the other Northern Routemasters but it retains the opening front upstairs windows not fitted to the Northern examples.

A bizarre Routemaster – or is it? In an attempt to adapt them for one-person operation, Northern General first rebuilt a withdrawn 1958 rear-entrance Leyland PD3 in 1972 to become a front-entrance bus. Known as the *Tynesider*, it was given a Routemaster-style bonnet and the driving position and upper deck were set back behind the engine. The bus was reregistered MCN 30K. A crash-damaged Routemaster was also rebuilt less drastically as the *Wearsider* with a set-back cab. Both had been withdrawn by June 1978. Taken at Percy Main in June 1977.

London Country Bus Services

On the formation of London Country Bus Services from 1 January 1970 the green RMLs, plus the RMCs and RCLs, passed to the new company. RML2457, seen at Uxbridge on route 347 to Hemel Hempstead, has had the new fleetname and emblem applied on its LT livery. 2 September 1972.

At first the LT green colour was retained, but with a yellow band and fleet numbers. Godstone garage's RML2314 displays the style in this view from 1972. The use of garage codes and running number plates continued from LT practice. (Photo by R. C. Riley/Online Transport Archive)

Traditional Green Line services were in decline, so an early decision was to end crew operation as soon as possible with an order for ninety AEC Reliance coaches (RP class). The RMC and most RCL buses were displaced to bus work by 1972, replacing the ageing RTs. RMC 1464 still retains the Green Line fleetname but is otherwise in bus livery as it works on route 330 at St Albans on 22 April 1972.

By 1974 National Bus Company standard livery of leaf green was replacing the LT colours, and RMC1507 at Romford on 11 September is so adorned. Romford market was an important regional shopping location at this time before the Lakeside Shopping Centre near Grays was opened, and the market day shoppers meant double-deck buses were a requirement on the 370.

In the 1970s, overall advertising had become popular in National Bus Company fleets and here RMC1516 has succumbed to the trend. It is promoting Fine Fare supermarkets (remember them?) while about to work a route 330 journey to Welwyn Garden City at Hemel Hempstead bus station in 1974.

The RCL class were displaced from Green Line routes 721 to Brentwood and 722 to Corbets Tey in 1972 by the new RP class. These were also then used on the 370, and RCLs 2239 and 2245 are seen inside Grays garage on 4 April 1976. These had not received NBC livery. LCBS retained three RCLs for Green Line route 709 to Godstone until May 1976.

Although not scheduled for Green Line work, green RMLs could sometimes be used as relief buses at busy times and this continued into LCBS days. RML2348 is at Windsor blinded for a relief turn on the 704 to London on 30 May 1976.

On Derby Day, special service 406F ran between Epsom station and the racecourse. Anything available could be drafted in to work on this busy service. On 6 June 1979 RML2349 from Northfleet garage leads a Leyland National and Atlantean arriving at Epsom Downs for the racecourse.

RML 2446 heads out of Dartford for Gravesend on route 480, 8 November 1979. At this time the 480 ran from Erith to Gravesend Valley Drive, an extension on from Denton acquired from Maidstone & District in October 1976. Leyland Atlanteans would replace the RMLs from November 1979 and RML2446 would be the last in service from Northfleet garage in February 1980.

London Transport Special Uses and Liveries

In July 1961 new RM664 was delivered in unpainted condition to test how this would wear in service. The silver appearance soon turned shabby and the vehicle gained standard red paint when it went in for overhaul in 1965. Similar experiments were carried out by Liverpool Corporation and South Wales Transport – at least around this time. This is seen when working from Highgate garage (HT) on route 276. (Photo by Harry Luff/Online Transport Archive)

London Transport RM1368 lost its upper deck in an arson attack on 31 December 1973. Rather than rebodying it, London Transport apprentices at Aldenham Works converted it to a single-deck vehicle with rear doors used by the experimental department at Chiswick Works, replacing RM8 which then went into normal service. It was an exhibit at a rally at Syon Park on 17 September 1978. This was the home of the London Transport Museum at the time, following the closure of the Museum of British Transport at Clapham and before the present site at Covent Garden became available. RM1368 was sold into preservation in 1990.

The British Airways Routemasters had become largely redundant following the extension of the Piccadilly Line to Heathrow. In 1975 thirteen were acquired by London Transport, numbered RMA1–13, and placed in service on Romford route 175 from October, replacing RTs. As they had no blind boxes, route boards were used. RMA5 is at Becontree Heath on 29 March 1976. Some, as here, were repainted red and carried advertising for the Round London Sightseeing Tour. Others retained British Airways livery. They proved unpopular with crews and were removed after a year, becoming driver trainers or staff buses.

The first overall advertising livery in London was applied to RM1737 in 1969 promoting Silexine Paint. Twenty-six RMs and RMLs received hand-painted adverts until 1976 including RM1255 promoting Rand Employment Agency. This was at Old Ford on route 8 on 30 March 1975.

For Elizabeth II's Silver Jubilee in 1977, twenty-five Routemasters were repainted in silver and renumbered as SRM 1–25. They were individually sponsored and carried exclusive adverts for their sponsor inside and out, as well as wool carpets. They were launched at an event in Hyde Park on 10 April, where SRM 18 (ex-RM1906) is seen with sponsorship by NatWest Bank. They were all taken off for repainting by the end of November. RM2 was painted silver in advance to promote the scheme to potential sponsors.

In 1979 London Transport marked 150 years of London Buses with a series of events and special liveries. Twelve Routemasters were painted in the livery of Shillibeer's original horse bus of 1829 and also DMS 2646 (the highest-numbered example, sponsored by British Leyland). RM2142 and the DMS are seen at a rally held in Battersea Park on 15 April 1979.

Shop-Linker was introduced on 7 April 1979. It was a circular service from Marble Arch to Oxford Street, Regent Street, Knightsbridge and Kensington. Sixteen Routemasters carried this livery, some with sponsored advertising as here. Originally the route number box displayed the flat fare of 30p, but this was removed after passengers confused the buses with those on route 30. The route was not successful and was withdrawn after 28 September. RM2207 was at Hyde Park Corner on 9 June.

Most of the AEC Routemasters which had passed from London Transport to London Country on its formation in 1970 were bought back by LT later in the 1970s as London Country replaced them with one-person-operated vehicles. Unlike the RMLs, the RMCs and RCLs did not go into passenger service but were used for training or as staff buses. However, while the shorter RMCs would continue in this role, twenty-six of the RCLs would be modified for service use on route 149 later in 1980, with the rear doors and luggage racks removed and the twin headlights replaced by single ones. They retained their two-piece front blind display. They were sent to Stamford Hill garage for route 149. RCL2242 crosses Lambeth Bridge on 26 September 1980.

The rear view shows that the rear emergency exit door was retained in the conversion. By 1984, all these had been taken out of service.

The Round London Sightseeing Tour in the 1970s was worked by a motley selection of vehicles including some of the latest DMS class Daimler Fleetlines, ex-Bournemouth open-top Daimler Fleetlines, FRM1 as previously mentioned, and hired coaches. Obsolete Fleet, Cheam, provided three former Northern General Routemasters. These were painted in London red and numbered RMF2761–3 following on from the last LT Routemaster RML2760. RMF2762, formerly Northern General 3091, loads on the stand at Victoria on 9 June 1979.

The royal wedding of Prince Charles and Lady Diana Spencer on 29 July 1981 was marked by eight sponsored Routemasters painted in this 'wedding gift' livery. A ninth, RM490, was painted to promote the livery to sponsors and was displayed at the North Weald Rally on 31 May.

In 1983, fifty years of London Transport was celebrated. Four Routemasters, RM8, 17, 1933 and 2116, were given pre-war-style liveries in slightly varying styles. RM17 was seen here at Victoria station on 7 July with black cab window surrounds, which were later repainted white.

Appropriately enough RM1983 was selected for commemorative treatment and was given gold livery. It was seen at an Open Day at Stamford Brook garage held on 4 June, one of many special events held during the year. It retained the livery until early 1984.

Ninety-seven of the 100 LCBS RMLs came back, and these were repainted and put into passenger service. In this view at Hyde Park Corner in April 1984, former green RML2412 has received an overall advertising livery, one of three RMLs that received adverts that year. Note the positions for the fleet number and roundel.

London Transport Training, etc.

While the RMLs would go into normal passenger service, the RMCs (and initially also RCLs) did not, being employed as training vehicles or staff buses, often retaining the green liveries they were acquired in. They worked on training duties alongside the RTs until these were all withdrawn. A rather battered RMC1491 stands alongside RT2926 as they take a layover break at Waterloo on 24 June 1978. Note that they both carry adverts for drivers – recruitment was becoming more problematic.

Forty-five RMCs came back to London Transport. RMC1480 is in National green at the Open Day held at Aldenham Works on 25 September 1983. Another example, repainted red, can be seen behind. In those days adverts were pasted on rather than inserted into framework, and it is evident where the adverts have been removed.

This view shows RCL2234 in training use at Bexleyheath garage at the end of 1979.

RML 2221 was an exception because in 1979 it was converted into a mobile cinema bus for the 150 years of London Transport events, for which it was also painted in the 'Shillibeer' livery (see p. 29). By 1981 it was repainted red with yellow lining, as seen here at the rally held at the Ensign Bus premises at Purfleet. It later became an information bus and was in use as such in 1999.

By 1983 all RTs had left LT service except RT1530, retained as a demonstration bus on the famous Chiswick Works skidpan, on which all drivers were trained. This was in use when an Open Day was held there on 3 July 1983 as part of the fifty years of London Transport celebrations. The normal skid bus at this time was RMC1518, also seen taking its turn on the wet. The Open Day offered the public the unique experience of travelling on the buses (lower deck only) as the drivers demonstrated their skills on the skidpan.

As well as the Routemasters bought back from London Country, London Transport also bought the front-entrance Routemasters that had been operated on behalf of British Airways before the Piccadilly Line was extended to Heathrow. These, including the thirteen that had been used as buses at Romford during 1975–6, soon became trainers or staff buses. RMA 4 was seen at the North Weald Rally in June 1985. Here the public were offered the chance to drive a bus for a small fee, and the instructor can be seen giving instructions, the bulkhead window and stairs behind the driver having been removed.

In the 1980s some RMs were already being withdrawn as one-person operation expanded. Here RMs (and an RMA) stand cannibalised for spares at Aldenham at the Open Day on 25 September 1983.

In order to promote export sales of redundant RMs, RM1288 has been fitted with an offside staircase and tropical sliding windows. It was displayed at the Showbus Rally held at Woburn on 2 September 1984.

In Service with London Regional Transport/London Buses, 1984–1994

In 1984 some Routemasters on route 23 were given tween-decks promotional advertising displaying the tourist locations served by the route, the only one serving Tower Hill. RML 2437 passes this location on 22 September 1984.

From May 1985 route 23 became the 15 and was promoted as a tourist route. Upton Park garage painted six RMLs with yellow roofs as a local initiative. This is seen to advantage on RML2527 as it waits on the stand outside Paddington station on 17 May 1985. This is also one of the buses fitted with an illuminated off-side advertisement panel.

The all-yellow roofs did not find favour with LT management, but a yellow strip on the roof and route branding was applied to three buses including RML2402. Note the yellow section on the blinds denoting whether the bus is routed via Bank or the weekend deviation via the Tower of London.

A new 'Bus It' campaign to promote tourist routes was introduced in 1988 on several Routemaster routes plus Titan-operated route 25. RML2682 displays promotion for route 38 listing two of the key places served – Piccadilly and Islington. It also displays the new roundel style adopted by London Buses in 1987 and the London Forest district name and tree emblem. This was at Hackney Central in 1990.

A simple form of displaying the main route points on route 23 is carried by RML2623 in Bishops Bridge Road, Paddington, on 29 July 1992. The bus is in a somewhat scruffy condition and the chromework around the radiator has gone. It is a hot day and the wind-down windows and opening cab window have all been deployed.

London Central RM1104 at Paddington with the second of the promotional styles used on route 36, which was also adopted for route 12. 2 May 1995.

While some London Buses Routemaster-operated routes were given route branding, South London went a stage further by adopting this red and cream livery for their route 159 in 1994. RM6 heads down Whitehall on 12 February 1994. Route 159 would become the last to operate Routemasters, the final day being 9 December 2005. However, by then vehicles were in standard red. South London had been sold to the Cowie Group who in turn became Arriva in 1997 and adopted standard red livery in line with the 80 per cent red dictat by then in force.

To mark the launch of the London General unit, two Routemasters, RM89 and RM1590, were painted in 1989 in a pre-war style similar to that worn by some buses in 1983 to mark fifty years of London Transport (see p. 32), but with 'General' fleetnames. They were usually to be found on route 11, as with RM1590 at Broadgate by Liverpool Street station on 12 June 1989.

London United also marked their launch by repainting RML880, the prototype RML, in this former tramway livery and renumbering it as ER880, its original intended number. It is shown here at a rally in 1994.

The first of London Buses' 'low cost' units, Stanwell Buses, trading as Westlink, took over routes 116, 117 (merged with 116) and 203 from 9 August 1986 using existing Leyland Nationals. While the basis of the livery was London red, white and blue bands were added. Westlink was the second London Buses company to be privatised when it was sold to its management in January 1994. It was then sold on to West Midlands Travel twelve weeks later and sold again to London United in 1995. Although Routemasters were not used in service, RM1681 was owned as a training bus and attended the North Weald bus rally on 18 June 1989.

The X15 was introduced in March 1989 as an express peak-hours route linking new housing developments in Beckton with central London. Rather interestingly it was worked by seven RMCs. These had last worked in East London on the old 723 Green Line route. They had not seen passenger use with London Transport since being acquired back from London Country, instead being used for training. East London gave them this attractive gold lining and later they received names. RMC1513 arrives at Beckton on the evening of 12 July.

In 1988 East London acquired two of the front-entrance RMA Routemasters. RMA8, which had last been with Bus Engineering Ltd as a staff bus, was treated to this coach livery. Though seen here at Addlestone in 1990 making a rally appearance, the blinds show its more usual duties working on the X15 alongside RMCs. When the X15 was converted to Leyland Titans in 1991, the RMCs and RMAs worked on the 15 alongside RMLs.

When the RMLs were refurbished from 1992, RML2760 was not included (along with RML903) because of its historic significance as the highest-numbered Routemaster. Here it is at Tower Hill on 19 March 1993 carrying exclusive advertising for the Ordnance Survey bicentenary. It remained at Upton Park, passing to Stagecoach on privatisation. It would last there until the end of Routemasters on the 15, then passing to Bow for the 8 until that ended. It was then retained as a heritage vehicle until placed on long loan to the London Bus Museum in 2013.

In 1991 London General's RML2516 was fitted with the doors from RMC1484 and renumbered DRM2516, becoming part of the special purposes fleet and used on route 11 until 2000. Here it was attending the Cobham Gathering in April 1993. DRM2516 remains in the Go-Ahead Commercial Services fleet in 2023 but the present vehicle is largely reconstructed from RML2283 and it now carries registration WLT 516.

Sightseeing with London Buses

A complete rethink of the tourist bus service took place in 1986. As tourists regarded the Routemaster as the iconic London bus it was decided that these should be used on the sightseeing tour rather than the latest vehicles or hired buses. Routemasters were available as they were being removed from suburban routes in favour of OPO vehicles. The tour was renamed 'The Original London Transport Sightseeing Tour' (TOLST). Six of the RMAs were also transferred to the sightseeing fleet in 1987 and this is RMA25 at Tower Hill on 9 October 1987.

London Buses also acquired twelve of the former Northern General Routemasters in 1979–80 but they were sold in 1981 without ever being used. However, EUP 407B, which had previously been hired from Obsolete Fleet, was added to the London Coaches fleet as RMT2793. Now open top, the former NGT 3090 looks smart in its London red livery as it crosses London Bridge on 23 August 1987.

From April 1989 the Sightseeing Tour became operated by the London Coaches operating unit. As tourists preferred open-top buses (despite the vagaries of British weather), twenty RMs had been suitably converted. RM1864 pauses on London Bridge, where top-deck passengers can photograph Tower Bridge and HMS *Belfast*. 18 March 1990.

In order to cater for disabled passengers, RM307 and RM450 were fitted with wheelchair lifts in 1988. The double-door access for this can be seen in this view of RM450 attending the British Coach Rally, held at Southampton on 23 April 1989.

In 1986 eleven RCLs formerly on route 149 were transferred to the Sightseeing fleet. New doors, air-operated by the driver, were fitted for winter use. In 1990 ten of the RCLs were converted to have removable centre sections to their roof. RCL2243 passes the Law Courts in Aldwych on 7 July 1991. All had public address equipment fitted.

To increase capacity, especially as most passengers wanted to travel upstairs in sunny weather, London Buses created the ERM (extended RM) class of ten open-top buses in 1990. Making the most of the versatility of the Routemaster design, with its front and rear sub-sections, an extra bay from withdrawn vehicles was inserted into the middle of an RM. This made them longer than an RML and increased the seating from sixty-four to seventy-six. The modifications were carried out by Kent Engineering of Canterbury. ERM 80 crosses London Bridge on 26 May 1990.

Routemasters in Scotland

Clydeside Scottish was formed when Western Scottish was split up from 17 June 1985. Following deregulation, they introduced a large fleet of over seventy Routemasters. RMs 37 and 697 (VLT37 and WLT 697) stand in Glasgow bus station on 16 September 1986. The company came back under Western Scottish management from May 1989 and the Routemasters had gone by August 1990.

London Transport retained the longer RML class, but one vehicle, RML900, WLT 900, was sold to Clydeside as a wreck for spares. However, they rebuilt it to working condition complete with carpets and known as the 'Clydesider'. This then made the long trip south to attend the North Weald Rally on 19 June 1988 and also ran trips on London routes 13 and 26 the previous day.

Kelvin Scottish was another new company created on 17 June 1985 with areas and vehicles split off from Central and Midland Scottish. They bought forty Routemasters from London Buses to compete with Strathclyde in Glasgow. Initially they retained their London numbers. RM388 heads for Easterhouse in Glasgow on 16 September 1986. Many of their Routemasters were later renumbered and also reregistered when their original registrations were transferred to coaches to disguise their age. Another six came from Western Scottish (ex-Clydeside) in 1990 and seven from Stagecoach in 1992.

The third Scottish Bus Group company to buy Routemasters was Strathtay, another creation, on 17 June 1985, from parts of Midland and Northern Scottish. They bought twenty-five from London Buses in 1986–8. Their Routemasters operated in both Perth and Dundee. SR16 WLT 610 works a Perth local service on 21 May 1987.

Some Strathtay Routemasters in Perth carried this red Perth City Transport livery. SR1 WTS 225A (ex-WLT 943) was photographed on 13 September 1989. As seen here, this company also reregistered Routemasters.

Strathtay SR19, WTS 128A in a revised version of the fleet livery at Dundee on 12 September 1991. Most had been withdrawn by 1992.

The mighty Stagecoach empire started out in 1980 following deregulation with coach services and then local services in the Dundee area. Ten LT Routemasters were bought in 1985. Former Northern General RCN 699 stands in Dundee bus station on 12 September 1986. This had come via Stevenson, Spath, in 1986 and would later be reregistered EDS 508B.

With deregulation, Stagecoach started competing in Glasgow under the Magicbus name, a name they would revive later. As with Clydeside and Kelvin, Routemasters were the choice for competing on the Easterhouse services. 741 DYE displays the stripes livery that would soon become familiar all over Britain. 8 July 1987. Seven later passed to Kelvin Central (as it was by then known) in 1992.

Routemasters with New English Bus Operators

Some former National Bus Company fleets, now privatised, took Routemasters. Cumberland, now owned by Stagecoach, took 900–1, WLT 713, ALM 24B from London Buses in 1987. They also took 902–7 from Kelvin Scottish, again in 1987. These worked in Carlisle on route 61 where 903, ALD 983B is seen on 19 June 1992. However, all had gone by the end of 1993.

East Yorkshire bought twelve Routemasters for use in Hull from April 1988. The last three of these came via Lincolnshire who had obtained them with the takeover of Gash, Newark (see p. 57). The buses were painted in the traditional dark blue livery rather than the red/white then in use. No. 806, 271 CLT (ex-RM1271) passes the bus station on 24 May 1988. Five of the buses were later reregistered.

United Counties took sixteen Routemasters from London Buses in 1988 plus one via Stagecoach (Magicbus) from Glasgow. They were operated in Bedford and Corby. No. 705, 68 CLT (ex-RM1068) works in Bedford on 28 May 1988. Note the use of the 'Routemaster' name, route details and full use of the blind boxes. The side lettering reads 'We've brought back conductors for even better service.'

East Midland 980 WLT 980 came from fellow Stagecoach-owned company United Counties (No. 711) in 1989, initially on loan. This was seen at Crich on 20 May 1990.

Others followed, and two were painted in period liveries. These were both entered at the North Weald Rally in June 1991. NSG 636A was originally RM1164 (164 CLT).

Some of the remaining municipal fleets also took RMs. Blackpool's Nos 521–6 came in 1986. A further batch, Nos 527–31/3, came in 1988. The first batch received this elaborate livery style, simplified on the later batch. There is full use of the blind boxes and the fleetname 'Blackpool Transport' is underlined in early London style. No. 525, 650 DYE (ex-RM1650), runs along the seafront on 18 May 1988. All had Leyland engines.

One further Routemaster came in 1989. However, No. 534 did not come direct from London Buses but instead from Burtons Biscuits of Blackpool where it had been used as a staff bus. It retained the Burtons advertising livery as seen taken outside the Rigby Road garage on 15 September 1991. The Blackpool fleet was also heavily into overall advertising in the 1990s. No. 522 became an advert for Pontins and many of the tram fleet carried overall adverts.

Facing competition from local companies Tyrer and Pennine, Burnley & Pendle bought five Routemasters ex-London Buses, RM 2087, 2114/33/56/80, in 1988. They emphasised their London connection by branding them 'Eastenders' and naming them after characters from the TV *Eastenders* series. This is No. 186 CUV 158C *Dirty Den* at Burnley on 23 May 1988. All had been stored out of service by the end of 1991.

Southampton had only recently withdrawn the last of their own rear-entrance conductor-operated buses when they opted to bring in Routemasters to combat competition from Solent Blueline. No. 406, WLT 564 (ex-RM 564), is prominently lettered for duties on route 16 including a notice telling passengers to hop on at the back. 13 June 1987. Fifteen were acquired from London Buses in 1987, one of which (ALD 921B) was not used.

Nearer to London, Southend Transport acquired twelve Routemasters from London Buses in 1988. Two more came via Southampton in 1989. No. 107, WLT 993, is seen at the bus station on 21 April 1993. Southend also acquired RCL2256 via dealers Brackell, Cheam, in 1990.

Gash, Newark, was an old-established firm running services between Newark and Nottingham. After deregulation they also took on local operator Lincolnshire Road Car on Newark local services using three Routemasters. RM19, ALD 1990B (ex-RM1990), was typical of these which retained their London red livery. This was photographed on 6 July 1987. Gash sold out to Lincolnshire in 1989 and the Routemasters were passed on to East Yorkshire.

Pulfrey, Great Gonerby, near Grantham, ran RM1109, seen in Grantham on 9 July 1987. It was sold on for preservation in 1988.

Verwood Transport bought former BEA NMY 648E, later RMA11. This was at the Netley Rally on 10 July 1988.

Green Rover of Watford started a commercial Saturday service, 346, from 28 July 1990 using former BEA Routemaster KGJ 602D. Watford Junction, 23 March 1991.

Timebus Travel had route 73 at Watford in 1995 on which they used RMs 2156 and 2180, seen here on 16 March. Although no longer operating bus services, they continue to have a large heritage fleet including ten Routemasters and also former cinema/information bus RCL2221.

Initially a dealer based at Grays and Hornchurch, Ensignbus moved to Purfleet in July 1981. They gained the contract to dispose of London Transport's unloved Daimler Fleetlines. In the 1980s they became a major player in London Sightseeing work. Their involvement in LRT contracts started in June 1986 with route 145, and not surprisingly ex-LT Fleetlines were used. Other routes in East London followed. They amassed a growing collection of heritage vehicles which sometimes appeared on service. RM1549 was given fleet livery and is seen at Upminster on 5 August 1990.

Blue Triangle started up running Essex-tendered contracts and rail replacements, later branching out into London Sightseeing and LRT contracts. They also built up a large collection of heritage vehicles. RCL2239 was in use on a Central line rail replacement job at Mile End station on 3 October 1999.

Another seaside town to see Routemaster operation was Bournemouth, when Routemaster Bournemouth took on the municipal Yellow Buses in 1993, one of which can be seen behind No. 290, YVS 290, on 11 July 1994. Despite the name Routemaster Bournemouth did not just use Routemasters but also Leyland Atlanteans, Daimler Fleetlines and Leyland Nationals. Services ceased in August 1994 after the company faced financial difficulties.

The Routemasters had long gone when London Country was split into four parts in 1986. However, two of those successor companies would operate them. Kentish Bus gained RMLs with a London contract (see p. 76). London & Country (ex-London Country South West) took RM1183 from Southend in 1983, initially on loan to cover a vehicle shortage. It was repainted in standard livery, as seen here at a rally in April 1994, and then later in traditional LT Country Area green – the first RM so treated since RM2 when new. It was sold in 1996.

Black Prince, Morley, ran a high-frequency service between Leeds and Morley with a variety of vehicles notable for all having different variations of the red/yellow livery. Most were rear engine vehicles, but they did also have RM2060, ALM 60B seen in Leeds on 12 August 1997.

When Routemaster operation outside London was largely coming to an end, a new company called Reading Mainline started competing with the municipal fleet in July 1994. Eventually forty-four RMs came to be used on eight routes including No. 26, NRH 803A, taken on 4 April 1996. They sold out to Reading Transport in 1998 who retained but reduced the service until eventual closure in July 2000. The remaining RMs were then sold back to Transport for London, and after refurbishing returned to service in London.

In 1997 Merseypride were using former BEA Routemaster NMY 655E on a Liverpool Heritage Tour.

On 8 September 1986 the Scarborough and Pickering area of United was transferred to East Yorkshire Motor Services' control as new subsidiary fleet Scarborough & District. A number of vehicles were operated on a seafront service in this 'bow tie' livery including 819, formerly Kelvin Scottish 1933 and originally RM1110.

A remarkable rebuild of a Routemaster was this example with Shaftesbury & District. This started out as one of the short front-entrance vehicles for the BEA contract and was bought in 1992 for spares. The company rebuilt it themselves with an extra bay as per the ERMs of London Coaches. The original staircase was missing, and the bus was fitted with one taken from an Ailsa, located to the middle bay area. The rear air suspension was replaced by coil springs. The rebuild, numbered RME1, entered service in 2000 and was photographed at Brooklands in April 2001.

Imperial Bus Company, Rainham, was started by Mick Biddell, a former associate of Roger Wright in Blue Triangle. He was a board member of the original management of the Essex Ongar Railway when it began running a diesel service between North Weald and Ongar on Sundays in 2004. A connecting bus service to Epping was provided and worked by RM1641, seen at Epping on 2 October 2005.

RML2317 was reassigned within the Go-Ahead Group to Metrobus in 2004, where it was used on a link between East Grinstead station and Kingscote, then the northern terminus of the Bluebell Railway. It was given LT Country Area green livery but with Metrobus fleetname. This was it at Kingscote on 11 August 2007.

RML2317 passed to fellow Go-Ahead group company Brighton & Hove in 2009 who repainted it in the livery of predecessor company Thomas Tilling. On 13 June 2010 it was displayed on Marina Drive, Brighton, as part of the centenary celebrations.

Routemasters with London Sightseeing Operators

Since deregulation London Buses had faced competition on London Sightseeing tours. A number of new companies had set up rival services, in some cases after previously providing vehicles on hire to London Transport for the tour. New innovations like taped commentaries and 'hop-on, hop-off' were now available. The Big Bus Company started in 1991 with two vehicles and have been the most successful of the rivals, still going strong in 2023. Their fleet included three of the ex-Northern General Routemasters which they operated until 2018 and also RM272 seen passing St Paul's Cathedral on 12 October 1997.

Much-travelled former Northern General Routemaster FPT588C had already been on the rounds on the sightseeing circuit with Obsolete Fleet when it was acquired by Blue Triangle as RMO2118 in January 1987. It seems to be carrying a full upstairs load as it crosses London Bridge on 23 August 1987. It then passed on to the Big Bus Company in April 1992.

Premium Tours operated a pair of Routemasters in 2012 on behalf of Harrods. These were RML2621, seen in Fleet Street on 18 August, and RM1979. Both these buses plus five other Routemasters were listed as still being with the company at the beginning of 2023 but had all been sold by the end of the year.

Routemasters with Non-PSV Operators

With their iconic status, Routemasters have been popular with all sorts of non-PSV operators. Timothy Ashton Hospitality Buses' Epsom 'Unit 1' was a former Northern General Routemaster. Here it was on Marina Drive, Brighton, where it had been providing hospitality for the 1984 London to Brighton Historical Commercial Vehicles Run.

In use as a mobile bar for corporate events is former London Transport Green Line RCL 2250 with 'On the Green'. This has been supremely presented in Green Line livery, complete with authentic-style blinds and even the garage code plate and running number. A conversion to convertible open top had taken place when the bus was used on London Sightseeing work. Taken at Woodcote, Oxfordshire, in 2014.

Say it with flowers – and Routemasters. Interflora were using RM1417 to do just this when seen at the National Agricultural Centre, Stoneleigh, Warwickshire, in July 1988.

Millwall Football Club bought RML2304 and this was entered in the RM60 event at Finsbury Park during 2014. It was still owned in 2023.

The words 'Snog' and 'Yoghurt' do not normally feature together, but RML2711 was ready to promote this so-named product when parked outside the Festival Hall on London's South Bank in 2014.

This reregistered Routemaster was promoting Marie Curie cancer care in Guildford during February 2001.

RM1790 didn't travel far, as it became a playbus for the London Borough of Lewisham. Very little has been done to the livery other than adding some coloured spots. March 1993.

The 2004 film adaptation of *Harry Potter and the Prisoner of Azkaban* featured the 'Knight Bus', a triple-deck London bus. A triple-decker was made for the film from London RT vehicles, mounted on a Dennis Javelin chassis. As this would have been too high to run on public roads and promote the film, this Routemaster was adapted with vinyls to look like a triple-decker. RM275 was entered at the 2004 North Weald Rally.

The Coulsdon Old Vehicle & Engineering Society bought RML2284 and rebuilt it as this single-deck club bus with a centre entrance and eight seats. This was entered at the Alton Rally in 2006.

Perhaps the most bizarre Routemaster! RM110 was among the buses sold to Clydeside Scottish in 1986, but it was back in London by 1992. Smoke City Wheelers of Tottenham then acquired it and had it customised to this ultra-low format with *very* limited headroom on both decks. Upstairs, the seats now face inwards rather than forward. The cab must have been very cramped as well. This creation was entered to the 1993 North Weald Rally.

Routemasters did not just find new owners in the UK. At the RM60 Event in 2014, RML2663 was entered by its owners from Germany. To meet local height regulations a flat roof that can be raised up has been fitted. The bus beyond this, RML2698, had been entered by owners in Sweden where it was used as a party bus.

London Post-privatisation, 1994–2002

London Coaches was the first part of London Buses to be privatised in May 1992, going to a management buy-out. London Coaches introduced a new livery and fleetname for their vehicles. From 17 August 1991, before privatisation, they also introduced 'London Plus', a 2.5-hour, thirty-stop 'Hop-on, Hop-off' tour to compete with those offered by rival companies. ERM 242 passes St Paul's Cathedral in June 1996. When these were eventually withdrawn, they passed to Mac Tours, Edinburgh, for continued sightseeing work there.

Perhaps seen as a retrograde step, London Coaches applied overall advertising to some buses, a practice favoured by some rivals but eschewed by London Buses at this time. RCL2220 carried a promotional livery for the Tower of London when photographed in July 1996. Others carried advertising for McDonald's restaurants.

When the operating units were privatised, because their Routemasters ran into the Central London Zone 1 where 80 per cent red was specified, they all retained the red livery, but chose to interpret it in differing ways to stress their separate ownerships. The LT roundels were ordered to be removed following privatisation. At first there were a number of experiments with livery styles before the companies settled on a design. One that didn't get adopted was this Metroline version on RML2737 with blue mudguards and wheel hubs. Seen in Oxford Street on 3 August 1995.

The final version adopted by Metroline was one of the most attractive seen on a Routemaster. RML2431 rounds Marble Arch on 19 October 1995.

MTL London Northern chose plain red which looked particularly drab on their Routemasters as even the tween-decks band was not picked out in another colour. This example has also suffered the indignity of losing the RM prefix to its number and being reregistered, although at least it retains the chromework around the radiator – some had this painted over. RM29 was at Golders Green on 18 March 1996. MTL London sold out to Metroline in 1998.

London United adopted a livery style with white (originally a very pale grey) upper deck and roof and grey skirt, which considerably brightened up their vehicles. Routemasters, however, were painted in a more traditional style with a tween-decks grey band and grey wheel hubs, and the fleetname and logo were placed between decks at the front of the advert panels. RML2702 also carries route branding for route 94 in this view at Marble Arch on 14 March 2001.

Stagecoach chose to paint their Routemasters with a traditional cream band and the fleetname originally in gold. Later this style with the corporate logo was adopted. RML 2415 in Oxford Street has had the radiator grille chromework overpainted, which somewhat spoils the appearance. 16 June 2002.

FirstGroup bought the CentreWest unit. Local area fleetnames were used, such as Gold Arrow for Westbourne Park garage. RML2486 has the Gold Arrow name, FirstGroup logo and route branding for route 23 which incorporates a lot of 'First'. Trafalgar Square, 27 May 1999.

The Go-Ahead Group traded as London Central and London General. London Central RM875 is one of those bought back by TfL and refurbished by Marshalls. This was at Victoria station, route branded for the 36, on 28 August 2002.

Fifty buses (including fifteen Routemasters) were given gold paint or vinyl livery to mark Elizabeth II's Golden Jubilee in 2002. Amongst these was RML2750 with Arriva, seen departing from Victoria station on route 38.

Two companies won tenders for routes that were operated by Routemasters and took over the existing vehicles to operate them. From 24 April 1993 Kentish Bus took on route 19 Finsbury Park–Battersea Bridge along with its allocation of twenty-four RMLs which they leased. This was the first crew-worked route awarded to a private company. The RMLs received the Kentish Bus livery and very smart they looked too, with route details and no advertising. RML2452 is at Hyde Park Corner on 30 April 1993. Sunday services, however, were OPO using buses from their other London tendered routes.

In December 1993 BTS became the second company to take over a Routemaster-operated route when they took on route 13 with twenty-two leased RMLs. RML 2674 is at Trafalgar Square on 12 February 1994. Unusually, unlike the other Routemaster-operated routes in London, they also ran on Sundays until July 1996 when OPO buses took over on the Sabbath. Their livery was a more orangey shade than the normal London red and the buses carried route details between the decks. BTS were bought by the Blazefield Group in 1994, who renamed the business London Sovereign.

The Last Years of London Service, 2003–2005

The first of the remaining twenty routes to be converted to OPO was the 15 on 29 August 2003. This route had seen the use of three RMCs and two remained until the last day. These included RMC1461 which had been repainted to original Green Line livery in 1994 (despite TfLs now all-red policy). This is seen at Paddington on 23 August 1995. When the 15 ended, Stagecoach donated RMC1461 to the Cobham Bus Museum.

Making a debut on the last day was Stagecoach RML2456, which had been repainted in original Country Area green livery. This then worked on Stagecoach's other route, the 8, until that ended on 4 June 2004. On 30–31 May 2004 it and RML2760 were run over a series of routes served by the company, and it is seen at Wanstead on the 101 to North Woolwich.

By the time route 73 ended on 3 September 2004, the appearance of 'guest' vehicles on the last day had become customary, both Routemasters and other types. Some carried passengers, others just shadowed the route or carried invited patrons. Making a visit on the final day was RM1000, now safely in preservation and restored to original condition. This was its only appearance on a last day, and it is seen entering Oxford Street at Marble Arch. Another 'one-off' in public service on this day was the London Transport Museum's FRM1.

When route 19 ended on 1 April 2005, one of the guest vehicles was RML2665 of Stagecoach East London which had been painted in a version of the company's corporate livery. This had also performed on the last day of route 36 on 28 January 2005. Here it is seen in Finsbury Park.

In 2004, to celebrate fifty years of Routemasters, and also 175 years since the first Shillibeer horse buses, two Routemasters received commemorative liveries. RM25 received this scheme marking the Great Northern Railway horse buses of the 1850s, designed by students at the Central St Martin's College of Art & Design. This was passing Sadler's Wells on the final day, 1 April 2005.

The other repainted bus was RML2524 in this pseudo-Shillibeer livery. This was at Finsbury Park station on 25 July 2004.

Route 13 ended on 21 October 2005, ending Routemaster operation on this route after forty-three years. This had latterly been worked by London Sovereign with the RMs bought back by TfL and refurbished by Marshall. They carried this drab overall red livery. RM2089 is at Golders Green shortly before the end on 15 October.

The penultimate route was the 38 which finished on 28 October 2005. A highlight amongst the now customary array of 'guest' vehicles performing was RMF1254. Now preserved by Imperial Buses and restored to the form in which it worked on the BEA contract, it was loaned to Ensignbus for one round trip on the route. This was the first time in its career that it had ever carried passengers on a London bus route. I captured this in Piccadilly near Hyde Park Corner.

The 159 was the final route on 9 December 2005. On the preceding day there was a Running Day with a vast turnout of twenty-four 'guest' vehicles of all types, not just Routemasters. Amongst the participating vehicles was RML2565 of Ensignbus painted in traditional Stratford Blue livery. Ensignbus had expanded into Stratford-upon-Avon at this time. Three other Routemasters can also be seen in this view on Whitehall including one just visible in green.

The 159 bowed out at lunchtime on 9 December 2005. The last bus on the 159 was preceded by two duplicates from the Arriva fleet. These were RM5 and RM6, numerically the two oldest standard Routemasters which had remained in London service until the very end. RM5 had been restored to original livery and would be retained as part of Arriva's heritage fleet. This was photographed proceeding along Whitehall.

RM6 still carried the gold livery applied for Elizabeth II's Golden Jubilee in 2002. Note that this is carrying advertising for the two heritage routes that would continue with Routemaster operation (see p. 83).

The last in service. RM2217 worked the last journey on route 159 from Marble Arch to Streatham Hill (Brixton garage). This had been restored by Arriva London South for the occasion and would also be retained afterwards. I also photographed this in Whitehall. The open-top bus was for the media filming its progress throughout and there was a police accompaniment. Onlookers threw flowers, and a primary school class in Brixton waved Union flags as it passed.

'Heritage' Routes 9 and 15

Although Routemasters ceased being used in normal service in 2005, they continued to be used on two 'heritage' routes launched in November 2005. Stagecoach worked the 15 which paralleled the normal service between Tower Hill and Trafalgar Square daily from *c*. 09.30–17.30. RM 324 was seen at St Paul's Cathedral on 22 September 2008. Note the traditional London Transport livery and dedicated publicity for the London Transport Museum.

Heritage route 9 was worked by First London and ran from the Royal Albert Hall to Aldwych. RM1735 nears journey's end along the Strand on 17 June 2006. This route ceased to run in 2014.

Heading the other way along the Strand on 9 June 2006 is RM1650, alias SRM3. This had been repainted in 2004 in the silver livery it carried in 1977 for Elizabeth II's Silver Jubilee and used at the time on route 7. After the withdrawal of Routemasters from normal service this was retained and used on heritage route 9.

In 2008 RM1933 received this livery to commemorate 100 years of Bow garage where an Open Day was held on 28 June. It is seen having arrived at Tower Hill on heritage route 15 on 14 June. The route was reduced from every fifteen to every twenty minutes in November 2015. From March to September 2019 the 15 ran only weekends and bank holidays. It did not operate in 2020 because of the Covid-19 pandemic and when the contract expired in November 2020 it was not renewed.

'New Routemaster'

The first of eight New Bus for London hybrid LT class entered service on route 38 in February 2012. Built by Wrightbus and with design input by TfL and Heatherwick Studio, these were the production result of the London Mayor Boris Johnson's competition for a new bus to replace the Routemaster. Officially the 'New Bus for London', they were nicknamed 'Borismasters'. LT2 was at Green Park on 17 June. Note the registration – this would be changed later when the main production batches followed to put them all in a LTZ 1+ sequence. A total of 1,000 were built.

Routemasters Still in Service in the 2020s

Go-Ahead London maintain a Commercial Services fleet separate from their Transport for London tendered services. In 2023 this included five Routemasters – RM9; RMLs 2305, 2318 and 2604; and DRM2516 (fitted with rear doors). RML2318 is open top and is seen on 26 May 2023 at Victoria working on a shuttle service to the Chelsea Flower Show. The Commercial Services vehicles are not restricted to the TfL all-red livery specified for buses on tendered services.

Londoner Buses started on 15 October 2022 with a tourist route A between Piccadilly Circus and Waterloo station. The company had RMs 871, 1583 and 1941, RMLs 887 and 2290. RM1941 rounds Trafalgar Square on 4 May 2023. From 21 October 2023 route A became the T1 and a new route T15 began between Piccadilly and Tower Hill, thus recreating much of the former Stagecoach heritage route 15. Other Routemasters have been hired in for this.

A different approach to tourism is offered by Ghost Bus Tours Ltd. Trading as London Necrobus, they use Routemasters on their evening Ghost Bus Tours which visit places not on the other company's routes. They also operate similar services in York and Edinburgh, again with Routemasters. RML2516, seen among traffic in the Strand by Charing Cross station, promises to take travellers to Trafalgar Scare, Notting Hell and Earl's Corpse! 24 September 2016.

Brigit's Afternoon Tea Tours offers another different approach in that their buses – all Routemasters – have been fitted with tables and patrons are served afternoon tea and cakes while enjoying their tour. In 2013 there were thirteen RMs and RMLs in the fleet. RM1776 is used on the Paddington Bear tour – presumably marmalade sandwiches are served! This was seen on 26 July 2023 entering Park Lane at Marble Arch. Two others are used on a Peppa Pig tour and these have a toilet installed on the lower deck.

The Epping Ongar Railway reopened as a steam and diesel heritage railway in May 2012. As trains are not able to work into Epping station where both platforms are used by LUL, on operating days bus route 339 provides a link from Epping station to the railway at North Weald, with some journeys continuing to Ongar and (since 2014) Shenfield. The service is registered as a route so that local passengers can be carried as well. Former London Transport vehicles from the associated London Vintage Bus Hire Company fleet are used. The route number 339 is that of the original Country Area route which ran from Warley, south of Brentwood, to Harlow via Ongar and Epping. RM1993 stands at North Weald station on 10 June 2016 with dedicated advertising for the railway.

In 2022 London Vintage Bus Hire painted RML902 in this white livery specifically for wedding hire work. It was taken passing through Victoria amidst contrasting architectural styles on 27 May.

Preservation

The first Routemaster to enter private preservation was RM3. The Leyland-engined prototype was withdrawn by London Transport and acquired by the London Bus Preservation Group in 1974. Here it is seen at the old Cobham Bus Museum site in Redhill Road at the April 1980 Gathering. At the 1983 Gathering all four prototypes were lined up together for probably the first time at a public event.

The London Bus Preservation Group have rebuilt RM3 with the original-style bonnet and radiator grille and revived the original number of RML3 (Routemaster Leyland). This was it at the RM50 event in Finsbury Park, July 2004.

The RM 50 anniversary held in Finsbury Park in July 2004 was organised by the Routemaster Operators and Owners Association to mark fifty years since the first Routemaster. London Transport Museum's RM1 is seen ahead of the numerical last Routemaster, RML2760. This at the time was part of the Stagecoach heritage fleet but was passed on to the London Bus Preservation Trust on loan in 2013. When RM50 was held some Routemasters were still in front-line service at the time.

Ten years on from RM50, RM60 was also staged in Finsbury Park. This impressive line-up of the type has RM2217 on the left. This, the highest-numbered standard RM and the last to work in daily bus service in December 2005, was retained by then owners Arriva as part of their heritage fleet, as shown on the advertising panel. In 2022 Arriva announced the end of their heritage fleet: 'It is with great sadness that Arriva London announces that our Heritage Fleet operation will cease at the end of 2022 and the vehicles will be available for sale for further use or preservation.'

After many years out of the limelight, the London Transport Museum returned RM2 to its original radiator style and green livery in time to feature at RM60. The fourth prototype, RMC4, has also been restored by owners London Bus Company/London Vintage Bus Hire to original condition as CRL4.

On 30 September 2014, the four prototypes plus FRM1 were posed together at Earl's Court to mark sixty years since RM1's first appearance at the Commercial Motor Show held there. RM1 has the final type of radiator as fitted to early production models. It is not considered possible to recreate the original 1954 front as the horizontal radiator was prone to overheating. (Photo: M. Batten collection)

The classic London Transport livery as many people will think of it – cream band and gold underlined fleetname. RM5 was restored to this form as part of the Arriva heritage fleet. Here it is seen on a Running Day to commemorate 100 years of route 76 on 20 July 2013. One of the Stagecoach Routemasters on heritage route 15, which was still running at this time, can be seen travelling the opposite way at St Paul's Cathedral.

One of many London Routemasters privately restored to original condition and complete with period posters is RM613 with RM613 Owners Ltd. This was taking part in the Running Day centred on Muswell Hill held on 7 November 2021 and photographed at Colney Hatch Lane while working on former route 134A.

On 25 November 2018, a Running Day was held over former routes 104 Barnet–Moorgate and 104A Barnet–Golders Green. The 104 was the route on which the first batch of RMLs, RML880–903, were employed when new in 1961. Several of the batch survive and here RML899, now registered 215 UXJ, leads RML900 and RML893 at Moorgate, Finsbury Square, while the back of another can just be seen having departed. All three of these are now with London Vintage Bus Hire.

Not all London Routemasters have been restored to original condition. RML2396 was sporting the route branding for route 12 it would have carried in the 1990s. RM2116, just visible alongside, is preserved in the livery it wore in 1983 for the fifty years of London Transport, at which time it was maintained as the showbus for Seven Kings garage (AP). These were at the 2013 Alton Rally.

RML2323 sports the short-lived bright green livery introduced by London Country shortly before individual liveries were replaced by the standardised National green. This was taking part in a Country Bus Running Day based at East Grinstead on 14 April 2013.

The Running Day on Romford routes 174 and 175 organised by the London Bus Museum on 25 March 2023 gave an opportunity for the preserved former BEA Routemasters to reprise their role on route 175 in 1975–6. KGJ 602D in original livery heads through Romford with the route 175 route board just visible in the nearside front window.

An event that has come to be associated with Routemasters is the annual Running Day to the abandoned village of Imber on Salisbury Plain. This was evacuated in November 1943 to aid soldiers training for D-Day and has remained part of the army training area ever since. RML2344 and RM613 were amongst the participants in 2015. Note the full use of LT-style blind displays. (Photo by John Stiles)

A number of the Northern General Routemasters have been preserved. No. 2120 visited the North Weald Bus Rally on 28 June 1998 and shows one of the livery schemes that was applied to these before National red was imposed.

Some RMs have been preserved in the livery of the operators who ran them after London Transport. RMs 1859 and 1990 are both in the livery of Reading Mainline and were together at the Alton Rally in 2019.

Seen at the RM60 event at Finsbury Park in 2014. Preserved London Transport RM66 is an interesting 'might-have-been'. Built in 1959 and withdrawn in 1987, it was then converted to a towing/engineering support bus by Lamming of Coulsdon. However, it was deemed too light for serious towing and after two owners, passed into preservation in 1996. Since 2010 it has been based at the Swansea Bus Museum. London Transport did convert one Routemaster to single deck, RM 1368, but not as a towing vehicle (see p. 27).

While many of the preserved Routemasters have been restored to represent an earlier stage of their working life, RM1005 is unique. This is owned by Peter Hendy, Baron Hendy of Richmond Hill, the former Commissioner of Transport for London. This has been fitted with a Euro-VI engine making it fully compliant with current London Ultra Low Emissions Zone (ULEZ) requirements. This is proudly noted on the advertising panel, as seen at Brooklands in 2022 when it was waiting to work one of the tours from the museum.

Classic London buses at a classic London location. Members of the Routemaster Owners Association have an annual get-together at the famous Ace Café at Stonebridge Park off the North Circular Road. Here in December 2021. RCL2233 is seen alongside green RML2440.

Acknowledgements, Bibliography and Further Reading

Thank you to John Stiles, Online Transport Archive and the London Transport Museum for the use of photographs from their collections.

Akehurst, Laurie, *London Country 2nd edition* (Capital Transport, 2001)

Blacker, Ken, *Routemaster* (two volumes) (Capital Transport, 1991, 1992)

Bruce, J. Graeme & Colin Curtis, *The London Motor Bus: Its Origin and Development* (London Transport, 1973)

Curtis, Colin H., *Buses of London* (London Transport, 1977)

Elborough, Travis, *The Bus We Loved: London's Affair with the Routemaster* (Granta, 2006)

Fennell, Steve, *London Country in the 1970s* (Ian Allan, 2003)

Lane, Kevin, *London Half-cab Farewell* (Ian Allan, 2009)

Morgan, Andrew, *Routemaster Handbook* (Capital Transport, 1992)

Rhodes, Mike, *London Routemasters in the Late 1970s and Early 1980s* (Amberley, 2020)

Rixon, Geoff, *Routemaster Heyday* (Ian Allan, 1997)

Rixon, Geoff, *Routemaster Jubilee* (Ian Allan, 2004)

Smith, Graham, *London Buses: A Living Heritage* (Silver Link, 2017)

Wharmby, Matthew, *Last Years of the London Routemaster* (Pen & Sword, 2023)

Wharmby, Matthew, & Geoff Rixon, *Routemaster Requiem* (Ian Allan, 2006)

Whiting, James et al., *Birth of the Routemaster* (Capital Transport, 2004)

Whiting, James, *Young Routemasters* (Capital Transport, 2020)

DVD   *Routemaster Heyday* (Online Video, 2005)
        Buses (Ian Allan/Key Publishing) Monthly magazine

Various publications, including fleet lists and newsletters by the London Omnibus Traction Society. This is the principal society for enthusiasts of London Transport and its successors, and anyone with an interest in the London bus scene past and present is recommended to join. www.lots.org.uk